Check out these other action comics produced by: Victory Comics

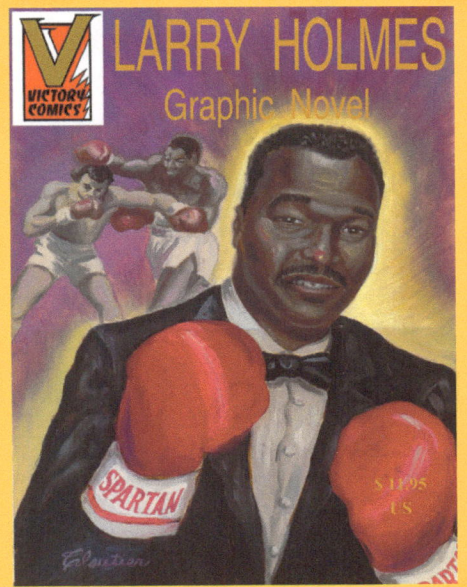

Credits

Artist: Tony Williams

Writer: Eva Stallings

Editor: Victoria Ward

Digital Layout: David Caywood

Floyd hated laughter because it was usually directed at him

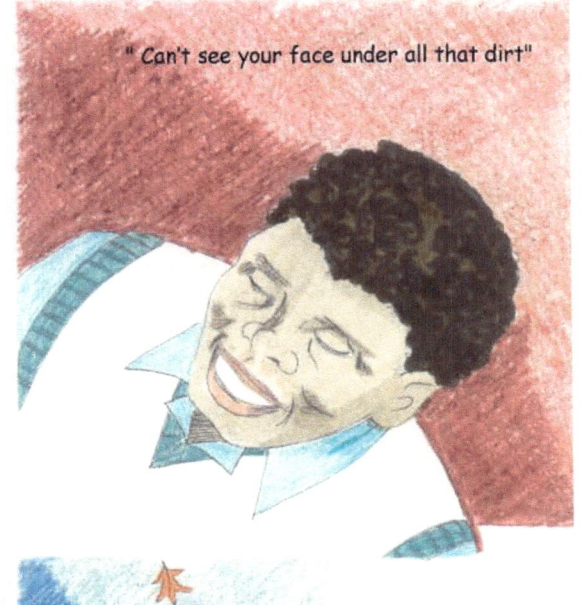

"Can't see your face under all that dirt"

"He's dumb, dirty and can't read or write"

It hurt Floyd to see his parents struggle so much; nine of them and one on the way. They moved from one cold water flat to another near a railway and not enough heat.

His Dad would get up early to light the stove.

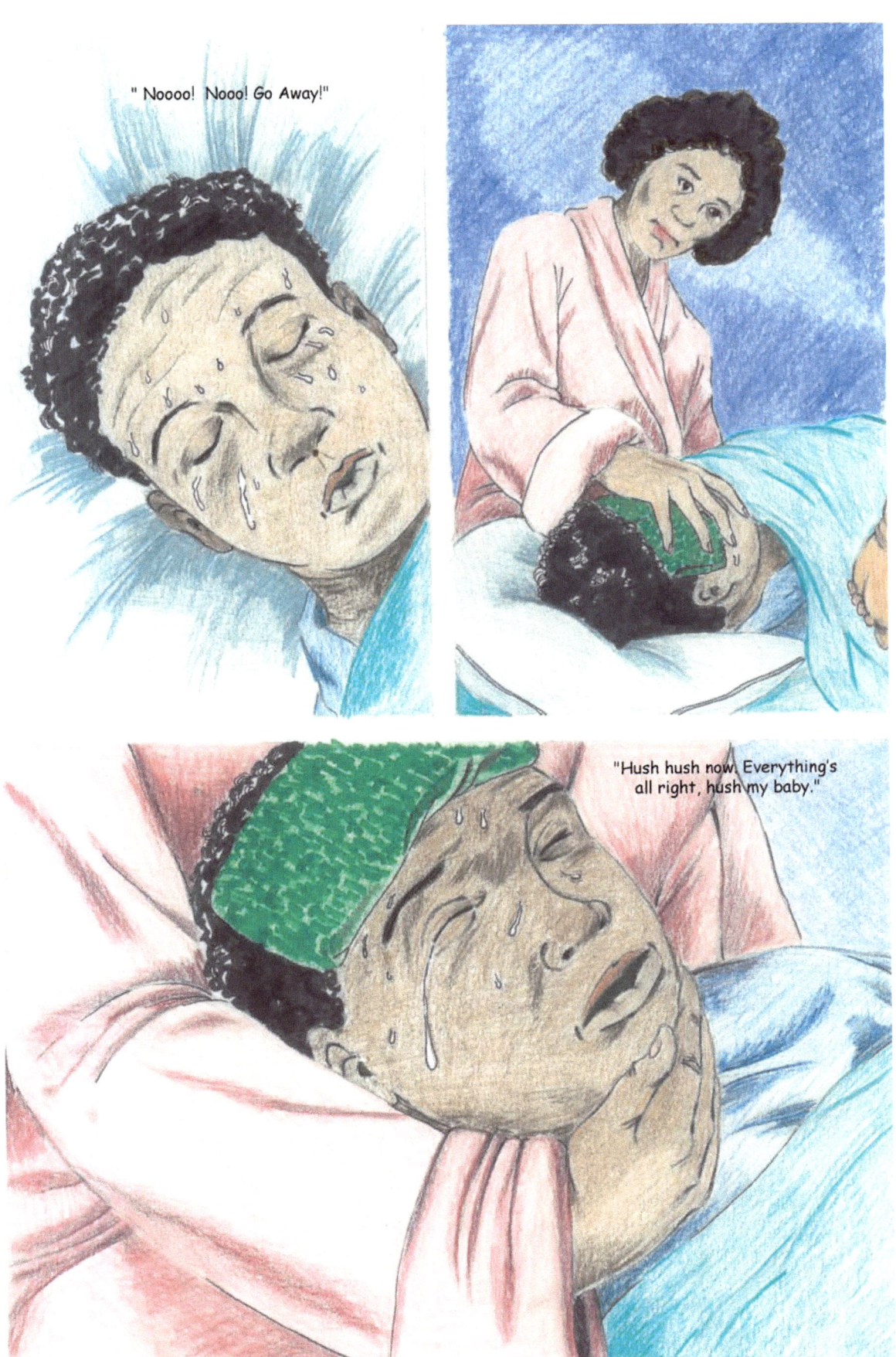

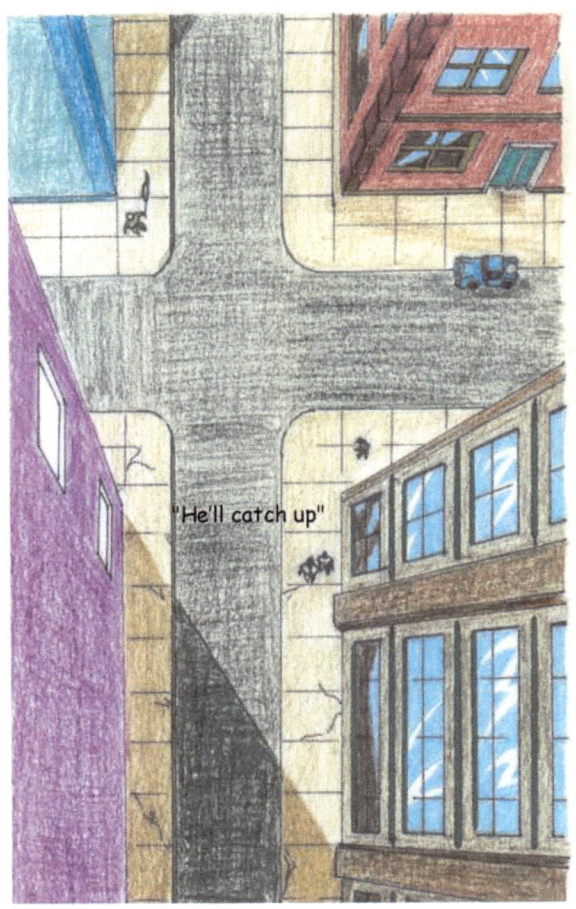

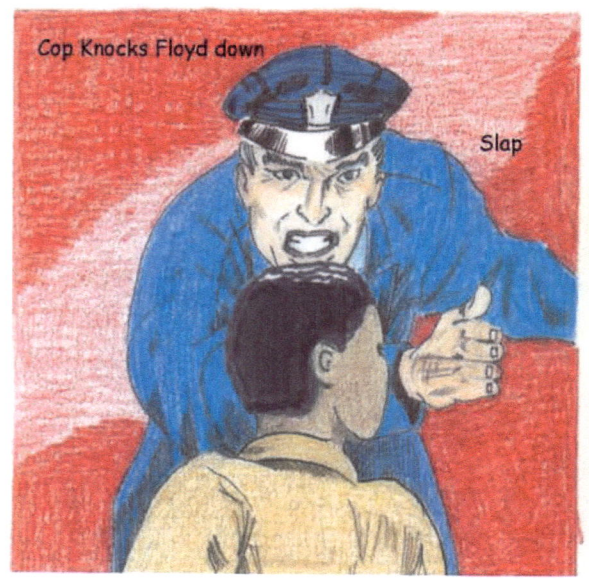

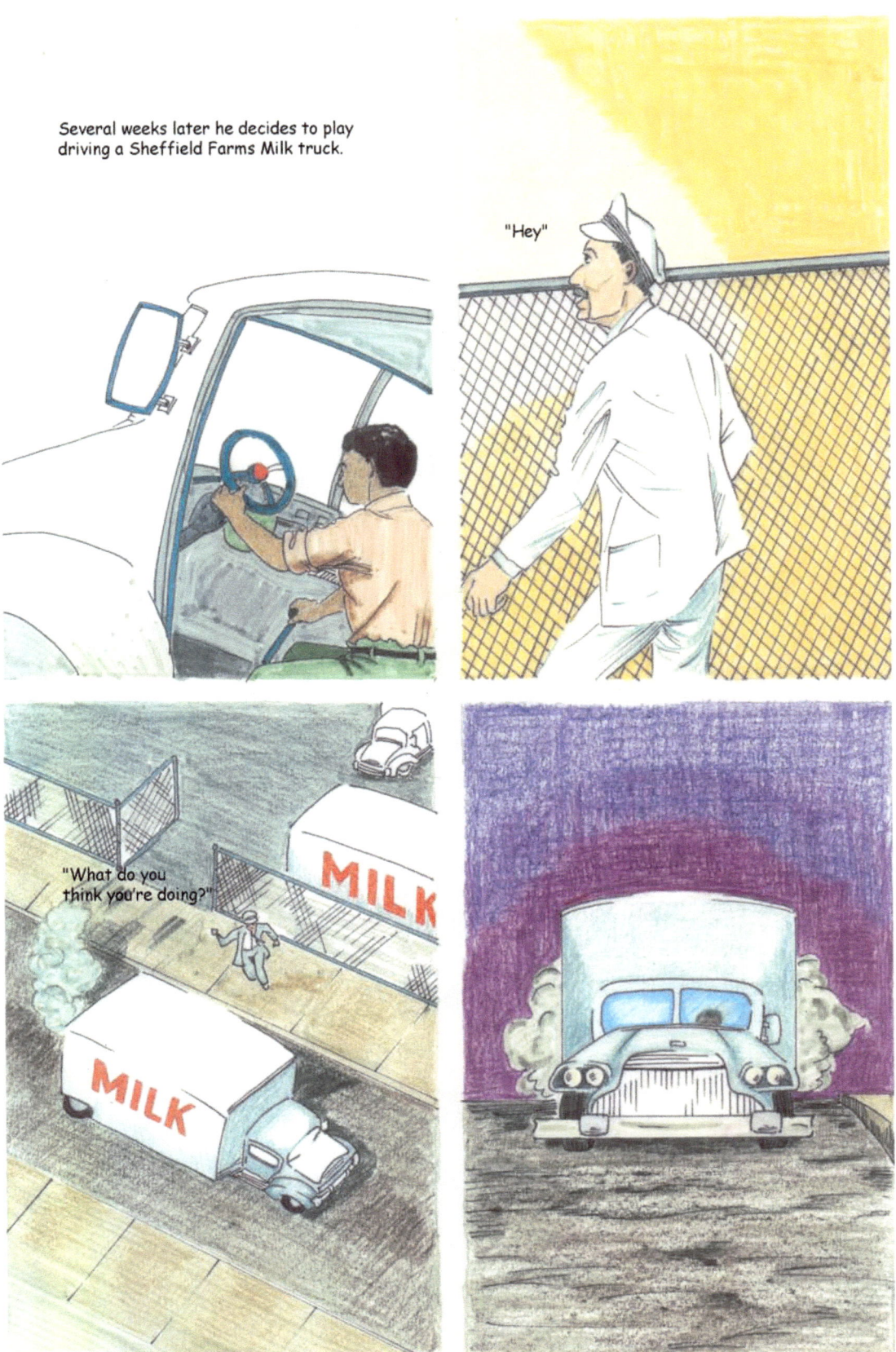

Wiltwyck School For Boys.

Floyd is shown into the dormitory. His cot is between the beds of Galento and Saunders.

In Wiltwych color didn't make a difference. Everyone got along. They argued, but never with a word about race. Never the way it was in Brooklyn.

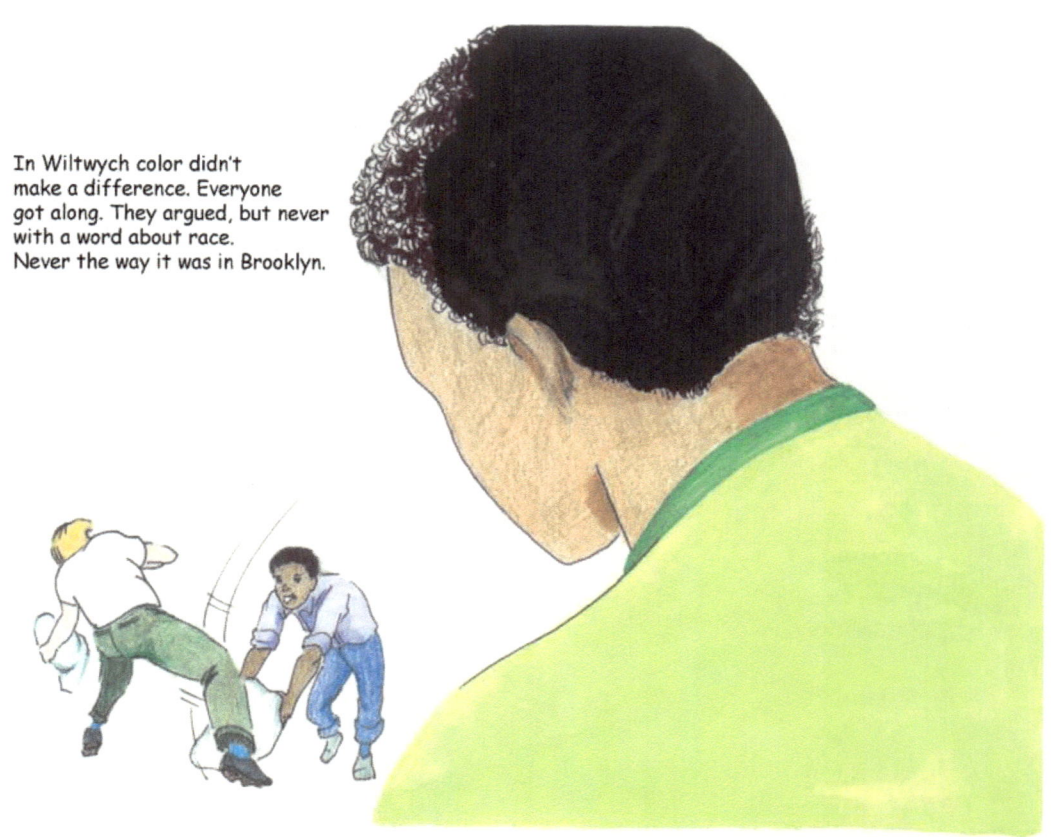

"Hey, Gimme back my pillow"

"Fat chance big boy, Come 'n get it!"

They chase each other but Floyd keeps quiet

"Aaaah! I'm hit, I'm dying, Patterson" "Haha-Wham you're dead!

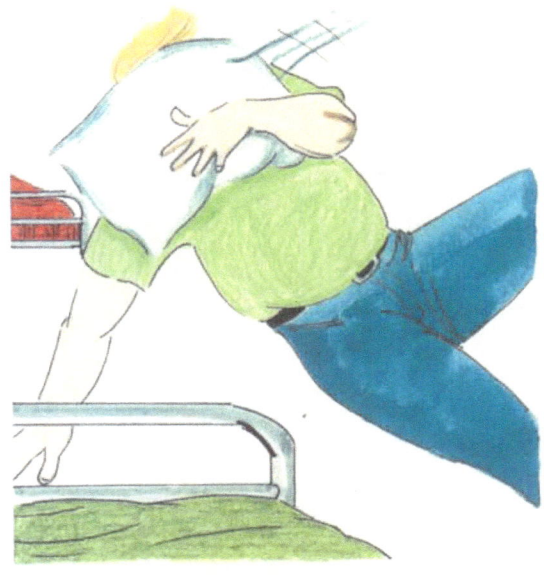

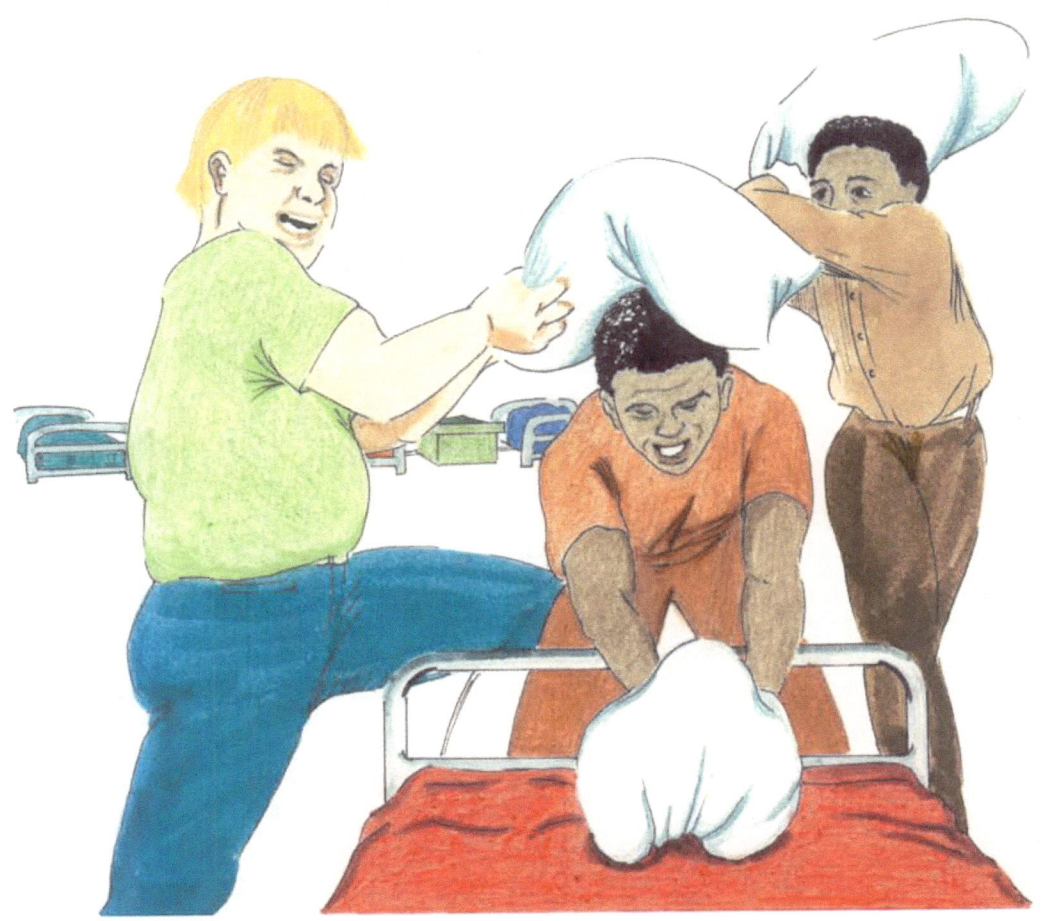

Children loved to watch Floyd box. Floyd would jump at an opponent while trying to throw a punch.

Floyd would miss and fall on his head. Kids would laugh, but he didn't mind."

Later sport writers called this my "gazelle punch"

Floyd is a little past fourteen when he starts going to Gramercy Park Gym with his brothers Frank and Billy. Frank Lavelle is training amateur fighters. Cus D'Amato sleeps there at night.

For six months, Floyd works out every day under the watchful eyes of Frank Lavelle and Cus D' Amato. He trains on the heavy bag, practices jabs, taking cover, how to shift his weight when he throws a punch.

Finally, Lavelle and D'Amato decide that Floyd is ready for his first amateur bout in January 1950. Floyd enters the sub-novice division of the 147 pound class, wearing the Empire Athletic Association colors. He has just turned 15. Floyd wins by default, since his opponent never shows up.

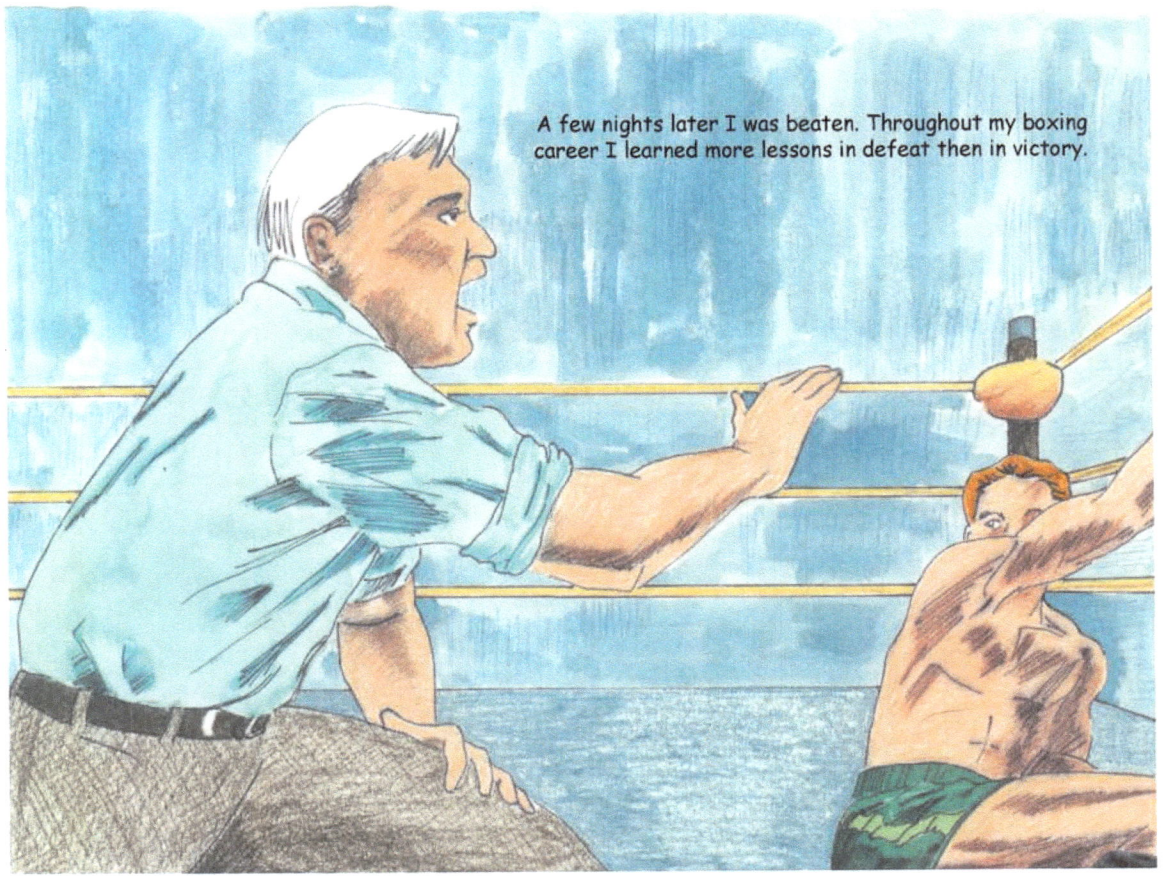

Floyd continues to fight as an amateur, all the while learning, learning, learning.

You're getting hit too often! Keep your hands up!

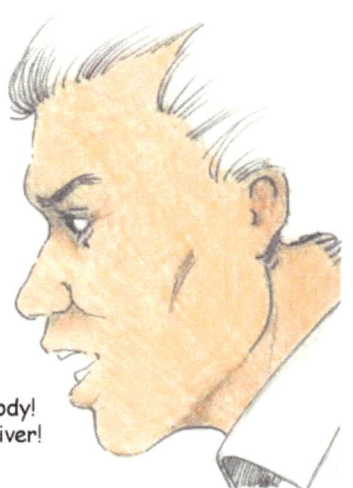

Remember: right elbow close to your body! You got to protect your liver!

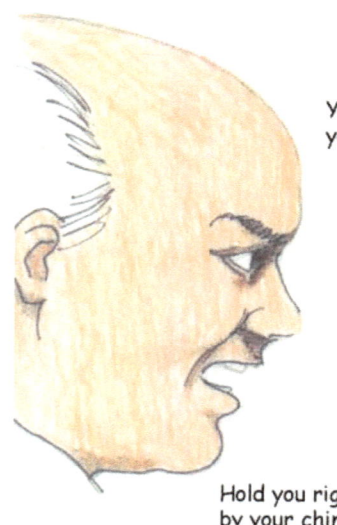

Yeah! If you get hit in the liver once, you'll remember it for the rest of your life!

Hide your chin behind your left shoulder! Now tilt your head – so any punch will be deflected!

Hold you right hand by your chin! Touch your earlobe lightly with the thumb of your glove. Keep your hands up!

"When a kid's young and wants to fight, all he thinks about is beating up the other guy. He doesn't realize the opponent has the same thought in mind. I had to learn how to avoid punches. That's where my so-called peek-a-boo defense began to take shape."

Floyd trains everywhere: at home, he shadow boxes with a rolled up news paper tucked under his right arm. If the paper drops while he is jabbing and moving, he knows that his guard was wrong.

To develop balance and a controlled eagerness, Floyd uses a "pendulum bag": a speed bag filled with sand, suspended from the ceiling on a rope.

D'Amato, Lavelle, Floyd's family and Mr. Schwefel manage to Convince Floyd to enter Alexander Hamilton Vocational and Technical High School. By the end of that year he realizes that an Olympic Gold Medal might be a fine entrée into Professional Boxing.

"When you are aimless, you never have any real direction. You never know what you're looking for. I was that way until I started to really think about the Olympics. After that, I knew which direction I needed to go."

Floyd had to fight 19 times to make the team - k.o.14, 4 wins by decision and one win due to default. He makes the team and wins the heavyweight gold medal of the 1962 Olympic games in Helsinki, Finland

"Nobody ever forgets his first trip overseas! For me it was more than that: every competitor on our team dressed exactly alike. I had to come 4,000 miles from home to really begin to feel that I was as good as everybody else."

Floyd gets his medal while the band plays Star Spangled Banner. Floyd sees Ingemar Johansson fight for the first time during finals.

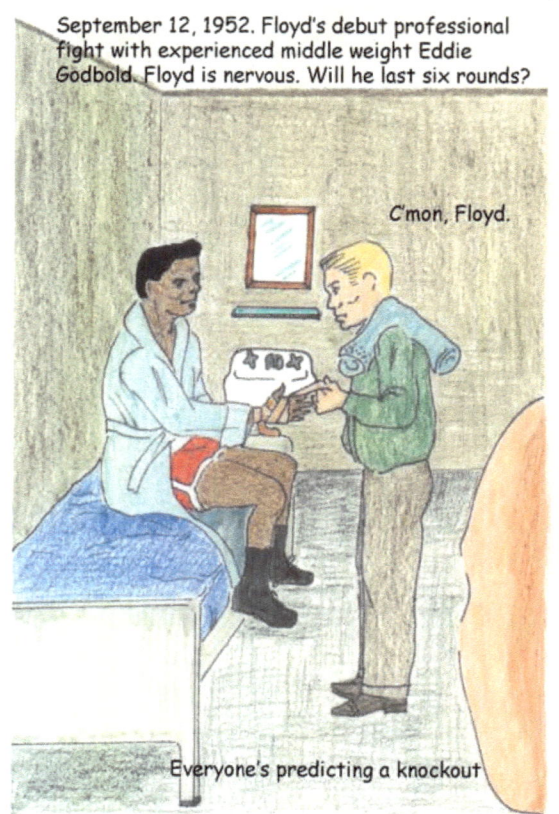

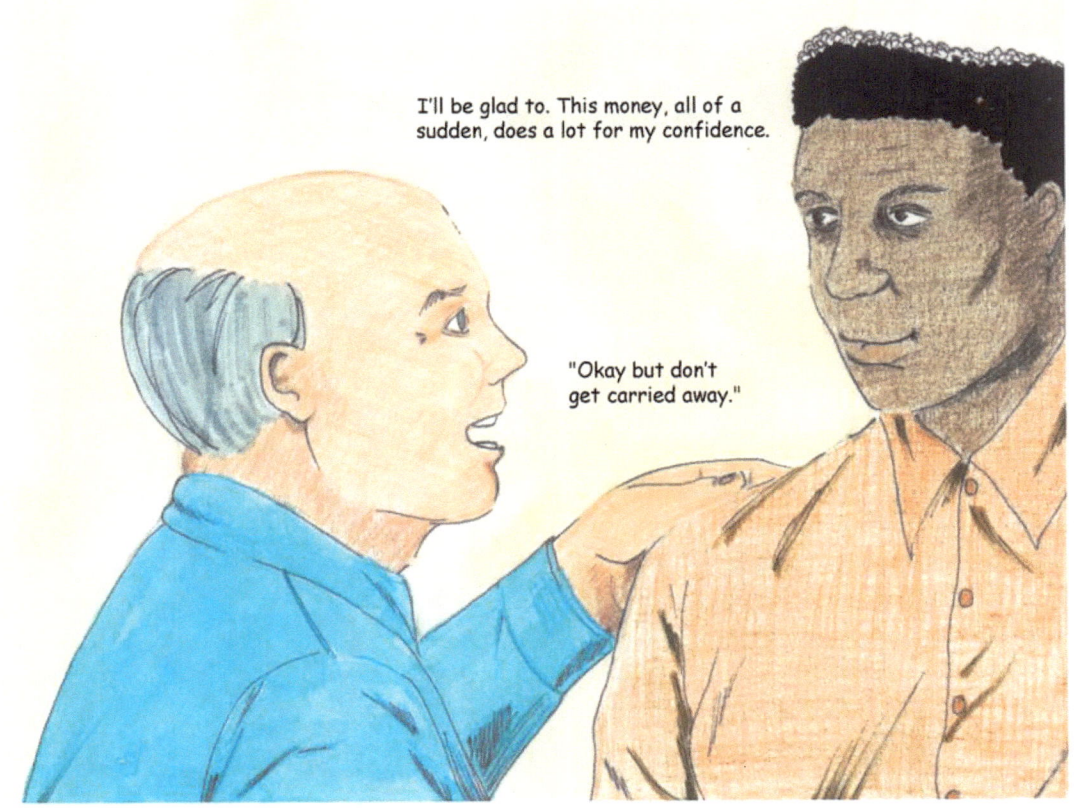

36

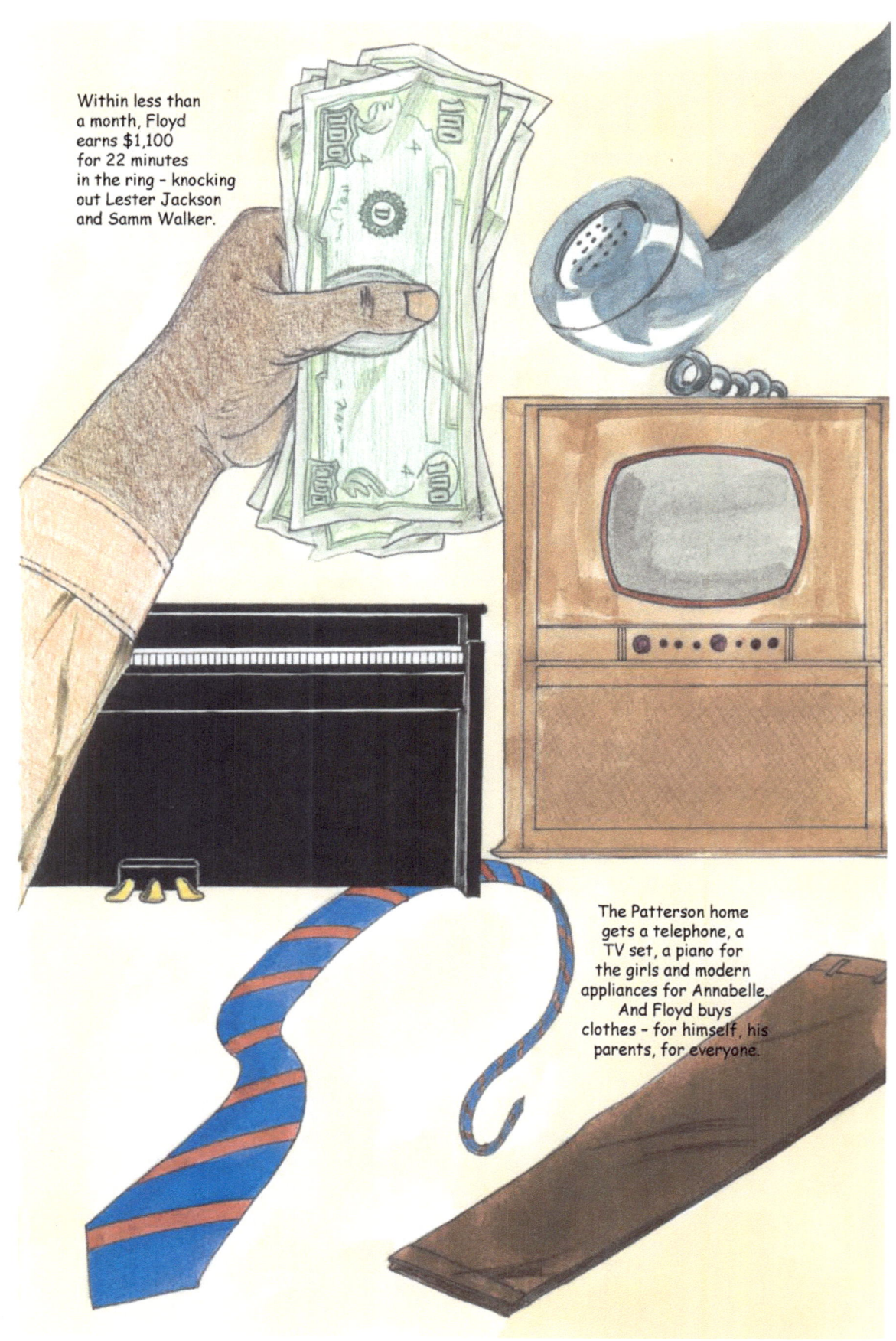

Floyd fights Lalu Sabotin December 29, 1952. His 4th straight K.O.

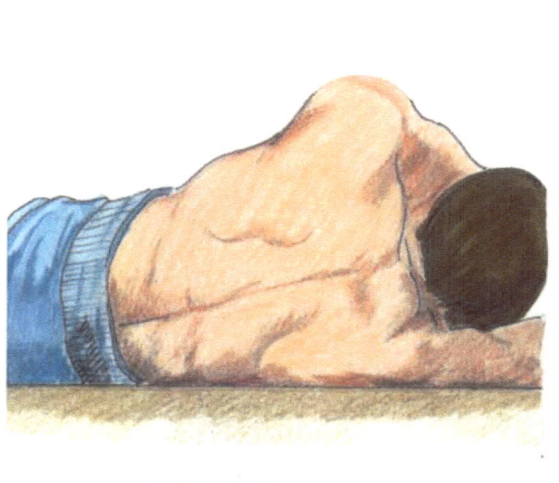

In Chicago fighting Chester Mieszala.

He loses his mouthpiece in a later round, after Floyd punches him.

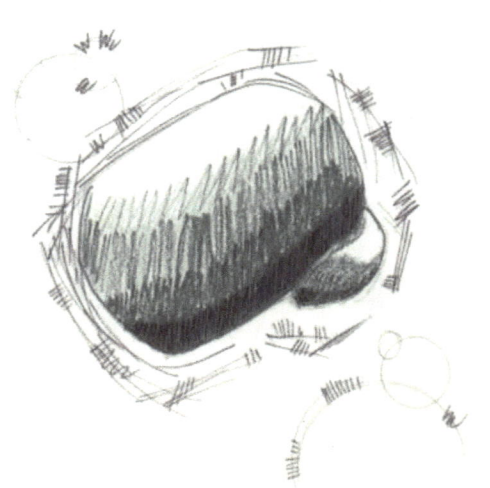

"Boxing is a sport. I am not vicious. I never wanted to be vicious. Many times, when an opponent was cut up, his face bloody, I laid off those areas of his face, and often I pleaded with the referee to end the fight. At the same time, I knew I was in the business of violence. After an 8 round fight with Dick Wagner, I couldn't eat anything but soup for the next three days."

fighter

Cus D'Amato is still "pacing" Floyd. He pairs his young fighter against Sam Brown, Yvon Durelle, Alvin Williams and Jessie Turner.

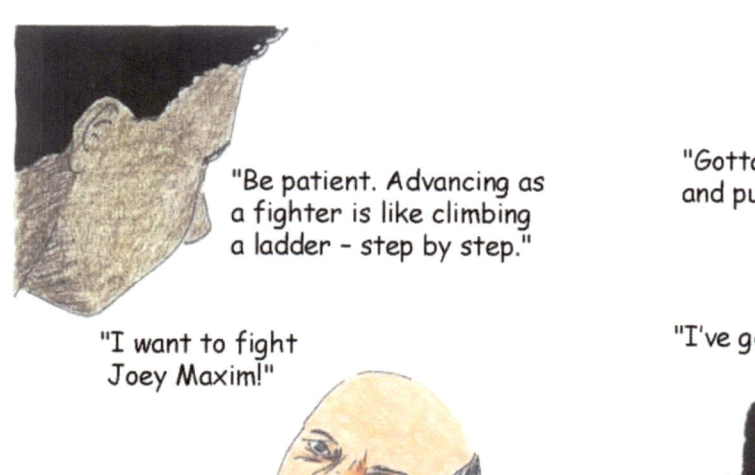

"Be patient. Advancing as a fighter is like climbing a ladder – step by step."

"Gotta have speed and punching power"

"I want to fight Joey Maxim!"

"I've gotten better, haven't I?

Floyd fights Maxim in an 8-rounder. He trains at Wiltwyck for the fight. Floyd loses although the Press thought he should have won.

His next opponent is Royer-Crecy. For the first time in his boxing career, Floyd experiences what it feels like to be knocked down.

"It was a strange experience. I have never been punched off my feet before. Cus tried to tell me that I slipped, but I knew that I had been knocked down."

On August 2nd, he faces his old sparring partner from Stillman's, Tommy Harrison. The referee stops the fight at 89 seconds.

October 11th Floyd meets Esau Ferdinand.

"Why don't you punch me??"

Floyd keeps on trying and wins by decision

"The only time I remember ever talking to an opponent during a fight was when I fought Ferdinand for the second time. In the 10th, I said to him: 'Why don't you punch me?', and then I knocked him out."

Next stop Madison Square Garden Main Event

Floyd wins by decision against Joe Gannon.

Floyd gets a $7,500 purse to fight against his friend, Jimmy Slade.

In 1954, Floyd earns about $20,000. In 1955, D'Amato predicts that Floyd would K.O. everybody. Floyd did, but he only fought 9 times, and most of the time away from New York.

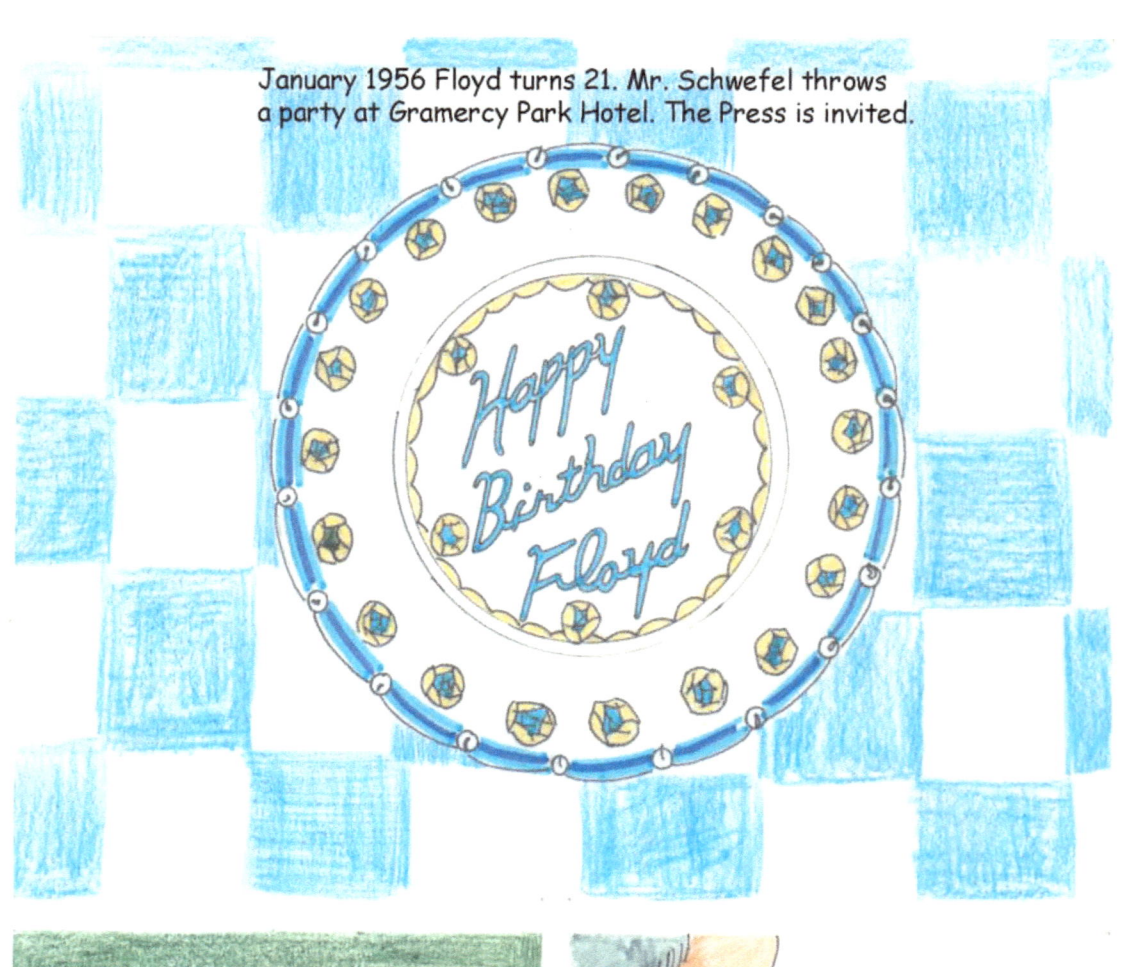

January 1956 Floyd turns 21. Mr. Schwefel throws a party at Gramercy Park Hotel. The Press is invited.

"Floyd is 21 today. From now on we are ready and willing to meet anybody."

"You mean Marciano too?"

"Anybody means anybody. He'll be in the heavyweight sweepstakes. We're challenging everybody - including Marciano, the Champion. We're after his title."

Rocky Marciano Knocked out Archie Moore in September 1955. In April 1956 Marciano announces his retirement.

Floyd and Sandra wed February 1956. He buys a house for his parents in MT. Vernon, N.Y. and a house for Sandra's family in Saint Albans. Later, Floyd buys his own house in Rockville Center.

"My mother could not get used to spending money. She picked the cheapest things she could find for the house, until I made her return everything, took her to the store and made her select things she liked without looking at the price."

Buster Watson joins Floyd as assistant trainer. Floyd and his entourage set up training camp at Kutsher's Country Club in Montecello to prepare for the fight against Archie Moore.

But an X-ray shows that Floyd fought Tommy "Hurricane" Jackson with a broken bone in his right hand. Fight is postponed until November 30th, to take place in Chicago.

Floyd trains at Sportsman's Park, a racetrack on the outskirts of the city.

For 6 weeks he does his roadwork on the racetrack.
Cus sets up a ring in the Grandstand Penthouse.

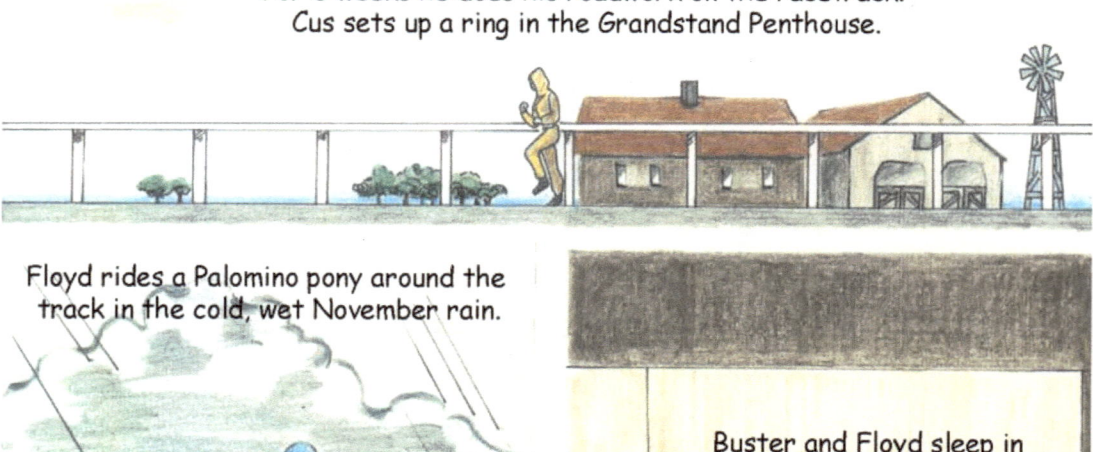

Floyd rides a Palomino pony around the track in the cold, wet November rain.

Buster and Floyd sleep in Jockey's quarters with Cus' bed barricading the door as he watches over his fighters.

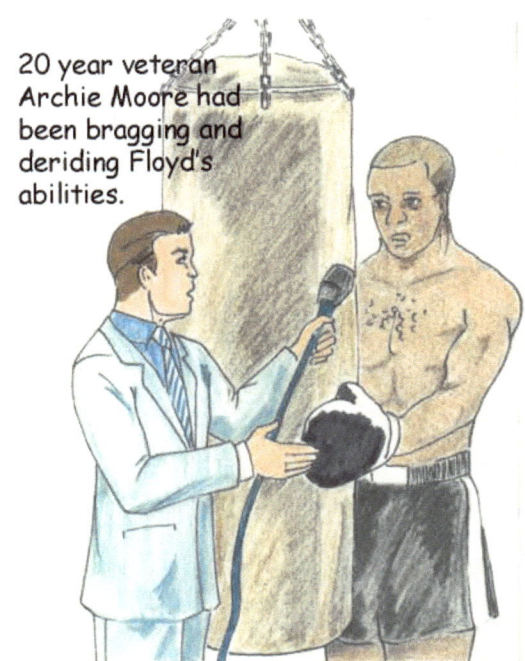

The Mayor of Mount Vernon gives Floyd a parade.

"Momma. I believe this is the first time I see you in all brand new things."

"I wish your teachers, Ms. Costen and Mr. Schwefel could be here."

"So do I Momma. They passed away before I could make them real proud of me."

"They always were proud of you."

I wanted people to be proud of me for who I was, not what I had become."

"Congratulations Floyd! Winning the title will open a lot of doors for you."

" Not in this town - they slam doors right in my face!"

"C'mon, relax. It doesn't matter."

"We started to call our segregated meals in our rooms "picnics". You can't walk around with bitterness in you, or sooner or later its got to turn into a pain that makes you want to strike out at the injustice."

"Once a fighter reaches his peak, he's got to keep going, otherwise he'll slip back. The heavyweight title is many things, one of which is a valuable piece of property. You work hard to get it. But you must work harder still to protect it."

Floyd is preparing for another title defense – against the Swede Ingemar Johansson. Seven years have passed since Floyd saw Johansson being disqualified in the 1952 Olympics.

Johansson's training camp is in an expensive private home in the Catskills.

"I lost interest in the fight against Johansson before e it even began. And I didn't realize it at the time."

The press keeps raving about "The Hammer of Thor" – Johansson's supposedly powerful right."

"Every fighter should be a little afraid of what could happen to him, because fear makes your mind sharper.
When you have nothing to fear,
your mind becomes dull."

"I never saw the big punch come at me. There wasn't any pain. Just shock."

"There was no feeling in me; just a kind of despair and numbness. I just lost."

"So your boy finally got it!" HA HA

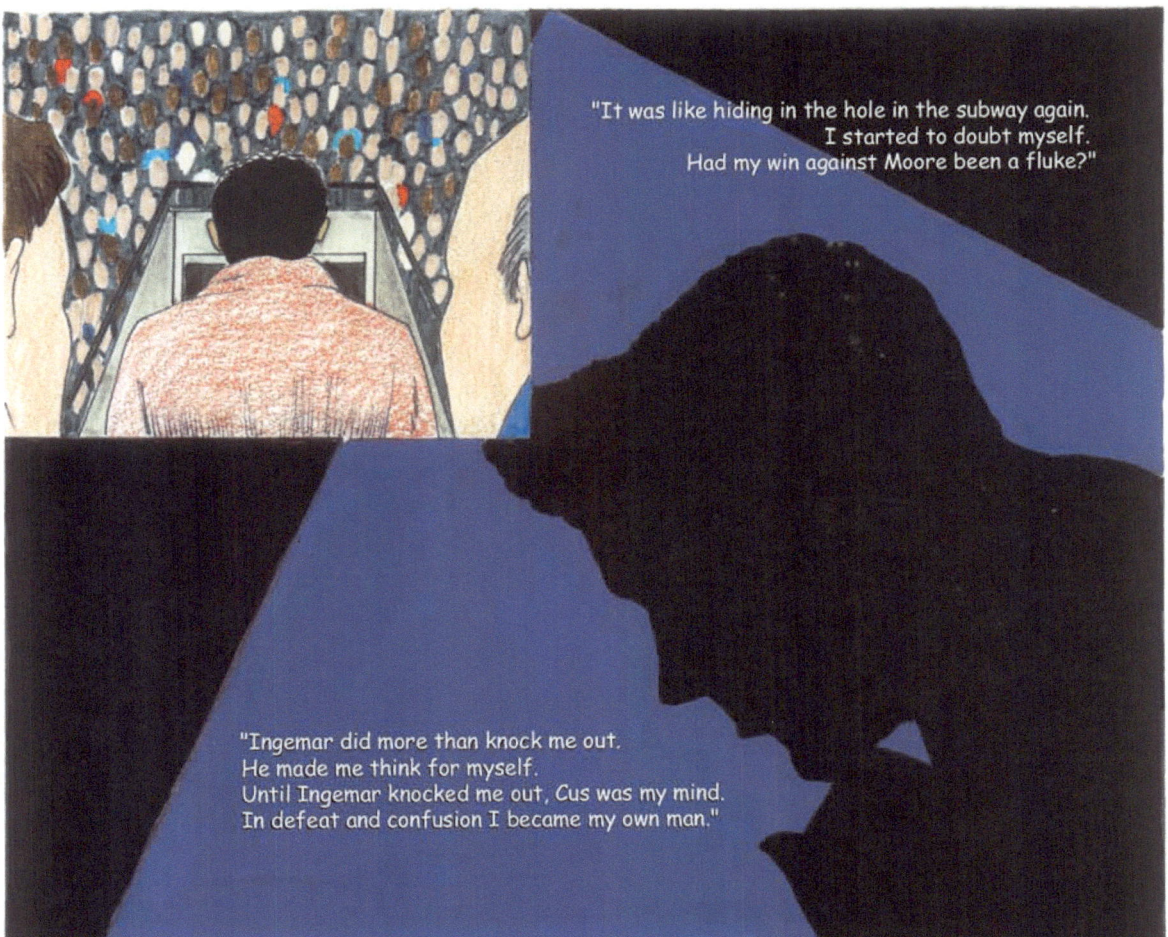

"It was like hiding in the hole in the subway again. I started to doubt myself. Had my win against Moore been a fluke?"

"Ingemar did more than knock me out.
He made me think for myself.
Until Ingemar knocked me out, Cus was my mind.
In defeat and confusion I became my own man."

Polo grounds – NYC –
June 20th 1960.

Floyd is utterly focused for this fight.

Hook to the left eye

"things were going to...

...be different this time."

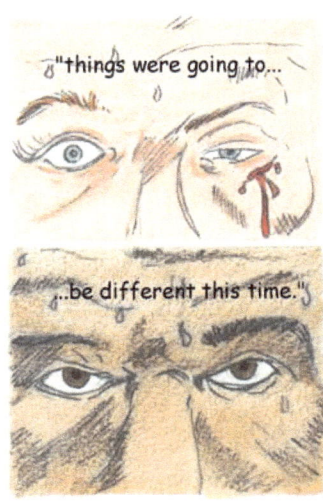

Floyd's grinning!

"Fighting is a serious business. I wasn't amused when I fought."

"I knew right then that I was

the Champion of the world again."

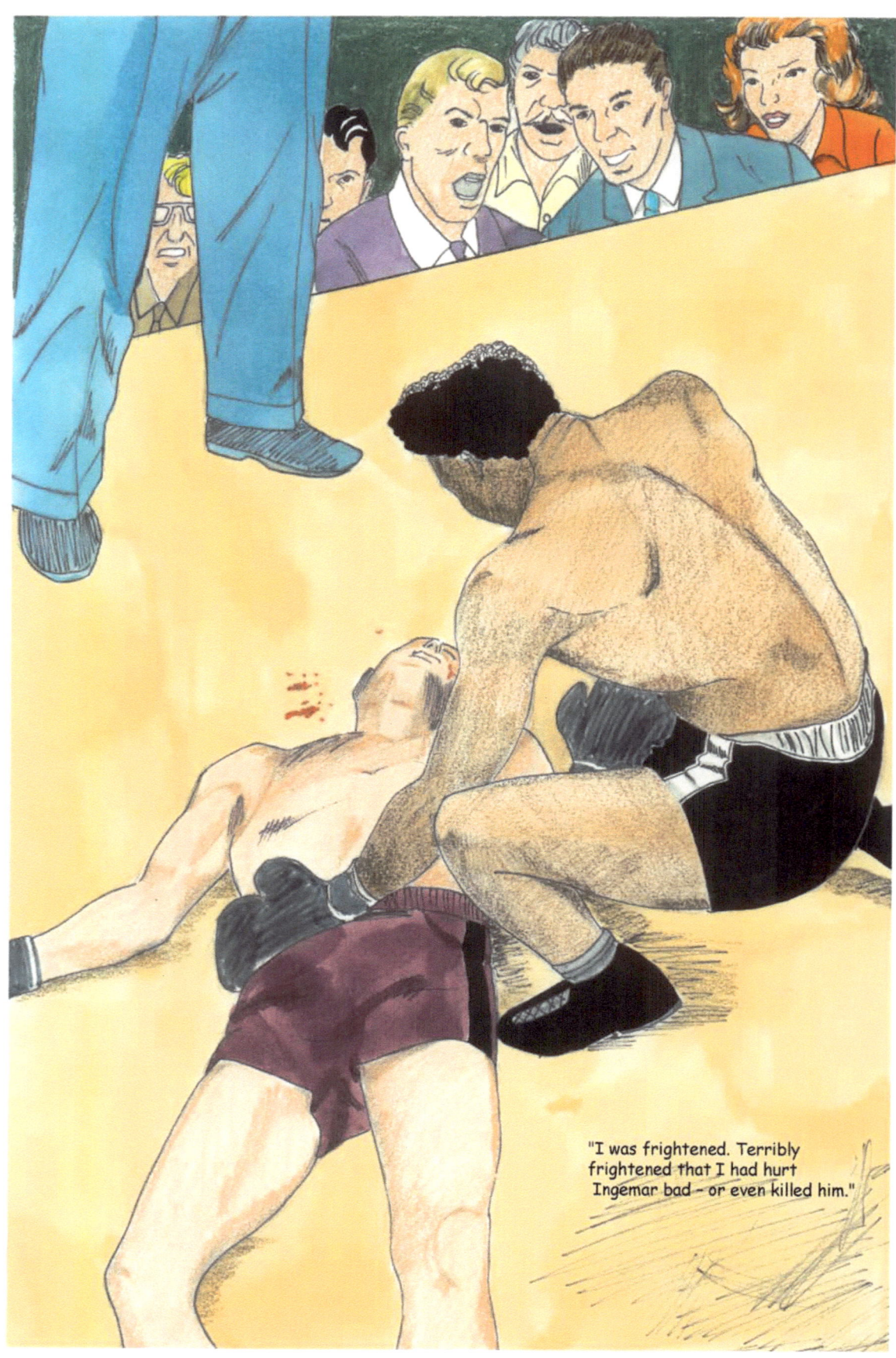

Floyd receives an official parade in Brooklyn. New York's Mayor, Robert Wagner declares a World Championship Day and presents Floyd with the city's medallion on the steps of City Hall

President Kennedy invites Floyd to meet with him in the White House. He is voted 'Fighter of The Year" by the Boxing Writers Association in 1960 and given the Championship Belt of "Ring Magazine".

"The preceding dark, wasted year took a terrible toll on my marriage. Soon after I won the title back, Sandra and I decided to go our separate ways."

March 13th, 1961 Floyd defends his title against Johansson, and December 4, 1961, against Tom Neely.

September 25, 1962, Sonny Liston snatches the title. Patterson reigned as the boxing heavyweight World Champion for 4 years and 305 days.

Floyd in a cockpit of a Cessna 172.
His 2nd wife Janet is navigating.

"Keep heading of zero-niner-zero. Traffic pattern demands a left downwind."

"There's our place! Doesn't it look pretty?"

"It sure does. You always wanted a farm."

1991 They come to train with Floyd and the Champ watches them with pride. Today Floyd is working with his adopted son, Tracy. The WBC declared that Tracy would have the opportunity to fight the titleholder in his weight class.

"Boxing is supposed to be a dirty business, but it has made me clean and enabled me to do some good for others. When I look at my boys, I can't help but think about the time when I was their age, how much I needed encouragement and comfort. I believed in nothing, least of all myself. All that has changed. When I wrote my book "Victory Over Myself" after my third fight against Ingemar, I ended it with the words: ".... I'm alone. Is there any other way?" Today, I know better: there is another way! But that's another story."

Easy to Learn

Carry Anywhere

Increase Your Enrollment with the Newest Solution for

Senior Citizens' Confidence, Fitness and Self Defense

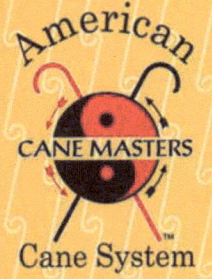

Featured on:
Wall Street Journal cover
CBS & Fox News   AARP Magazine
CNN Health Channel Readers Digest
AP Wire Service   PBS Network

We are getting over 100 calls a day from this publicity and...

We Need Schools & Instructors NOW!!

GRANDMASTER MARK SHUEY
Black Belt Magazine Hall of Famer

**Host a Seminar
Instructional Videos
Custom Hardwood Canes
Free Catalog**

800-422-2263
www.canemasters.com

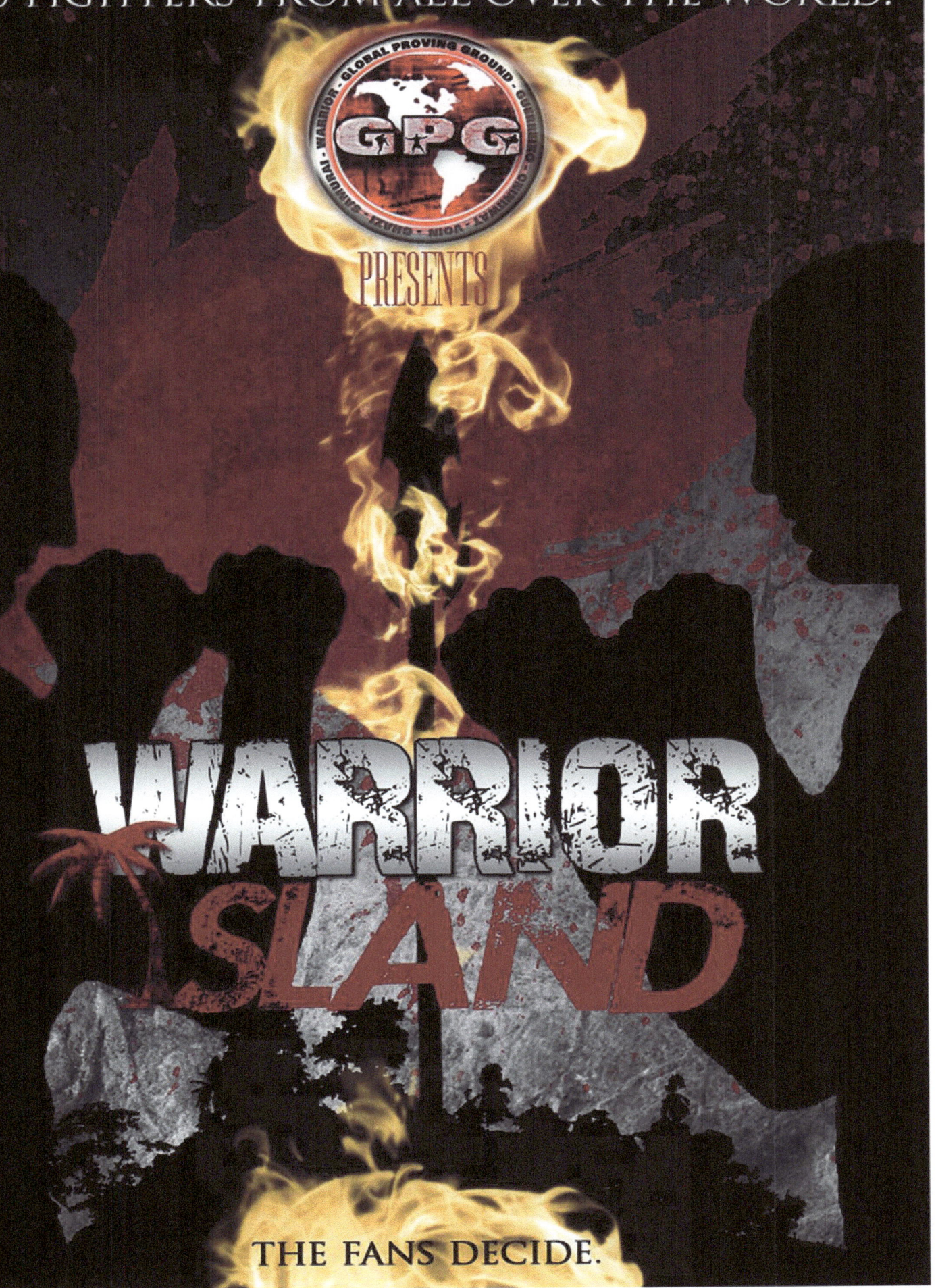

www.ingramcontent.com/pod-product-compliance
Lightning Source LLC
Chambersburg PA
CBHW060818090426
42738CB00002B/35